# Imagined Communities

Christian Boltanski
Sophie Calle
Denzil Forrester
Komar and Melamid
Giuseppe Penone
Tim Rollins + K.O.S.
Yinka Shonibare
Gary Simmons
Gillian Wearing

National Touring Exhibitions

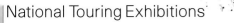

sbc

A National Touring Exhibition organised by the Hayward Gallery, London, in collaboration with Oldham Art Gallery

*Exhibition tour*
Oldham Art Gallery
*27 January – 24 March 1996*

John Hansard Gallery, University of Southampton
*9 April – 18 May*

Firstsite at the Minories, Colchester
*25 May – 3 July*

Walsall Museum and Art Gallery
*10 July – 25 August*

Royal Festival Hall, London
*7 September – 27 October*

Gallery of Modern Art, Glasgow
*6 December 1996 – 16 February 1997*

Exhibition organised by Andrew Patrizio *National Touring Exhibitions* and Richard Hylton *Oldham Art Gallery*

Education material for the exhibition prepared by Helen Luckett and Achim Borchardt

Catalogue designed by Paul Khera and Maria Beddoes
Printed by The Beacon Press, UK

Cover: image manipulation of *Holiday Camp* from *Picture Post*, 1946 (photo: C. Hewitt, courtesy Hulton Deutsch Collection)

National Touring Exhibitions, Hayward Gallery and Arts Council Collection publications are distributed by
Cornerhouse Publications, 70 Oxford Street, Manchester M1 5NH
Tel: 0161 237 9662 Fax: 0161 237 9664

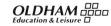

# Preface

National Touring Exhibitions engage visitors across the entire breadth of the United Kingdom, and this supports our belief in the exciting potential of a show based around the idea of community. The term 'community', and its interpretation in art, is one which deserves a new look, as it is clearly not only a word but also represents a fluid kind of reality.

An increasing number of artists have made sorties into the rich territory of community, and at their best they have respected both the integrity of their own working practices and the complexity of the communities with which they collaborate. Often they succeed in being rebellious and funny too. Part of the fascination with the topic may be seen as a response to the lingering legacy from Romanticism, which generated the idea of the artist as an isolated and visionary individual, at the opposite pole from community's sense of inclusion and participation.

We are glad that the new spirit of collaboration which lies behind the concept of *Imagined Communities* is echoed in the organisation of this project, which was first proposed by Oldham Art Gallery and developed in conjunction with National Touring Exhibitions. This exhibition represents a challenge to generally-held assumptions about communities and offers the opportunity of examining how artists have given voice to that challenge.

We should like to thank the artists and lenders who have made the exhibition possible. Their enthusiasm for the project has been particularly gratifying. Tim Rollins + K.O.S., Yinka Shonibare and Gillian Wearing have each created new work especially for *Imagined Communities*, whilst Komar and Melamid have offered us their *Most Wanted Paintings* series, via the Internet. We are grateful to the Dia Center for the Arts in New York, particularly Sara Tucker, for setting Komar and Melamid's Internet project on the information superhighway for us.

We thank Richard Hylton, Exhibitions Officer (Outreach) at Oldham Art Gallery, for proposing the idea and for developing the exhibition in such a considered and coherent way. We are grateful, too, to Kobena Mercer for his wide-ranging and thoughtful essay, and for his support and helpful observations throughout.

We are also grateful to the many people who have given valuable help and advice, especially the following: Ben Barzune, Claudia Carson, Eddie Chambers, Geoff Cox, Catherine Gibson, Tessa Gudgeon, Elisabeth McCrae, Virginia Nimarkoh, Maureen Paley, Philippe Rizzo, Francine Tagliaferro, Gilane Tawadros, Ron Warren; and to the International Initiatives Fund at the Arts Council of England, the North West Arts Board, the Institute of International Visual Arts, and Oldham Education and Leisure.

Henry Meyric Hughes
*Director of Exhibitions, Hayward Gallery*

Louise Karlsen
*Principal Galleries and Museums Officer, Oldham*

Andrew Patrizio
*Exhibition Organiser, National Touring Exhibitions*

# Introduction
## Richard Hylton

I said, I am that I am.
I am. I am. I am.[1]

*The fiction of the census is that everyone is in it, and that everyone has one – and only one – extremely clear place. No fractions.*[2]

On Saturday night 3rd September 1995, at Wembley Stadium, London, after twelve gruelling rounds of boxing, Frank Bruno beat America's Oliver McCall to become the WBC Heavyweight Champion of the World. Britain could at last celebrate the fact that it had a heavyweight champion. Well done, 'our Frank.' However, despite this victory, it can be argued that Bruno's talent lies more in pantomime than in the ring. Given his comparative mediocrity as a fighter, why is this eternally happy-go-lucky man so adored?

Bruno is a strange national hero. He is black, but he is a highly sought-after athlete and performer, and he is rich – quite different from the prevalent stereotype of his black male contemporaries. With his wife and family at his side, Bruno's persona does not threaten the nation's ideal image of itself; that is, the suburban family, 2.4 children playing in the garden with the dog. In fact, it is precisely because he is black that he is so well-loved. Bruno represents a 'safety valve.' 'I like Bruno' is a euphemism for 'I'm not a racist.'

And yet, what would have happened if Frank had spoken out against Paul Condon, the Metropolitan Police Commissioner who recently claimed that most of the mugging in London was perpetrated by black youth? Would he still be as popular? No doubt he would have won some new fans, but would he have lost his old ones? Being fixed within one community, or estranged from another, is by no means exclusive to Bruno, nor indeed to black people. It can happen to anyone who does not fit within the status quo or aspire to family values.

At the height of the Thatcher/Reagan era in the 1980s, Thatcher proclaimed that there is no such thing as society, only individuals. This statement came during a time which saw conflicts between the state and various communities, such as the miners and the disenfranchised black and white urban working class. Despite, or because of, the divisiveness of Thatcher's philosophy, people began to question openly the notion that communities fall into neat categories, not differentiated by class, race, or sexuality. The residual effect of this reckoning has been that not only can we no longer make assumptions about what exists across different communities, but also we can not assume to know what exists within them. The authoritative voice of the community has been undermined. This is the starting point for *Imagined Communities*.

Since the Enlightenment, artists have taken it upon themselves to travel the world, enter into unknown communities, and leave without trace, placing their subsequent work in a gallery and calling it art – no questions asked. This makes them no different from the documentary photographer who swaggers around, snapping an 'objective' view of society. From high art we go to the other extreme, community arts practice, which at times has had an equally problematic approach, thriving uncritically on the idea that art should be

4

for the benefit of the community, as a means of instigating social worth and change. The problem with both these approaches is that the community is seen as a homogenous mass, all difference redundant. This forsakes any complexities inherent in the term community, in pursuit of the rainbow-coloured melting pot.

*Imagined Communities* presents a variety of approaches to art production, from the figurative to the conceptual, in video, photography, sculpture and painting. In some cases, the work in this show was produced in the 1980s, at a time when some of the younger artists were still growing up. None of the works should be read as conclusive evidence of a place or community, or even wholly as the artist's own voice. They are best seen as fragments, or what Benedict Anderson refers to as 'fractions', of communities, society, people, and places – vignettes of our personal and public worlds.

Artists who make work with or about community seem particularly relevant today, as television continues to find new ways of providing 'everyone' with fifteen minutes of fame. In this exhibition the artists' work stands firmly opposed to this practice, which feeds our lust to see others publicly humiliated. Indeed, it is instructive to compare this work with the way in which television represents ordinary people through documentaries, game shows, video diaries, etc. Furthermore, the artists challenge the mystifying processes of art which are perpetuated by the notion of the singular authoritative voice. The resonance of this work lies in its willingness to address issues of representation, the role of the artists, and their positioning vis-à-vis their subject.

*Imagined Communities* intends to show how artists move across assumed boundaries, placing their feet in different camps. From the studio with Tim Rollins and K.O.S., we go into a community with Denzil Forrester, into the private domain with Sophie Calle, out onto the street with Gary Simmons, down the digital highway with Komar and Melamid, and back again with Giuseppe Penone, Christian Boltanski, Yinka Shonibare, and Gillian Wearing. Together, they suggest a sense of dislocation, mirroring ongoing fragmentation within the artistic community. Individually, they probe our assumptions about the certainty of community.

Notes

1  The title of this introduction is taken from the lyrics of the song *I am that I am*, by the late Peter Tosh, from his album *Equal Rights*, 1978

2  Benedict Anderson, *Imagined Communities: Reflections on the Origins and Spread of Nationalism* (London, Verso, 1983), p. 166. The title of this exhibition is indebted to Benedict Anderson's book which informed the ideas behind its presentation

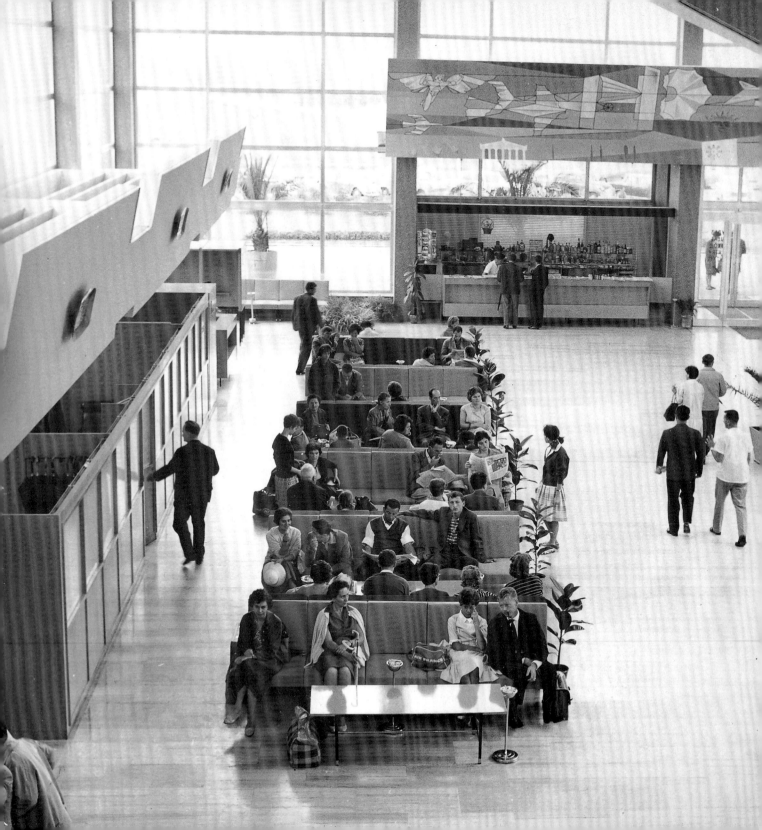

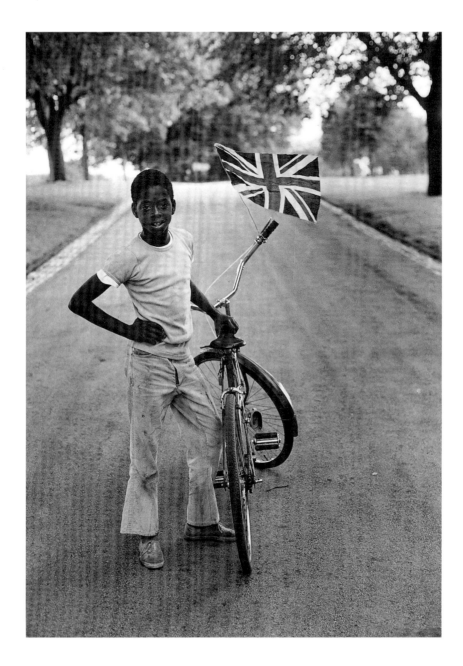

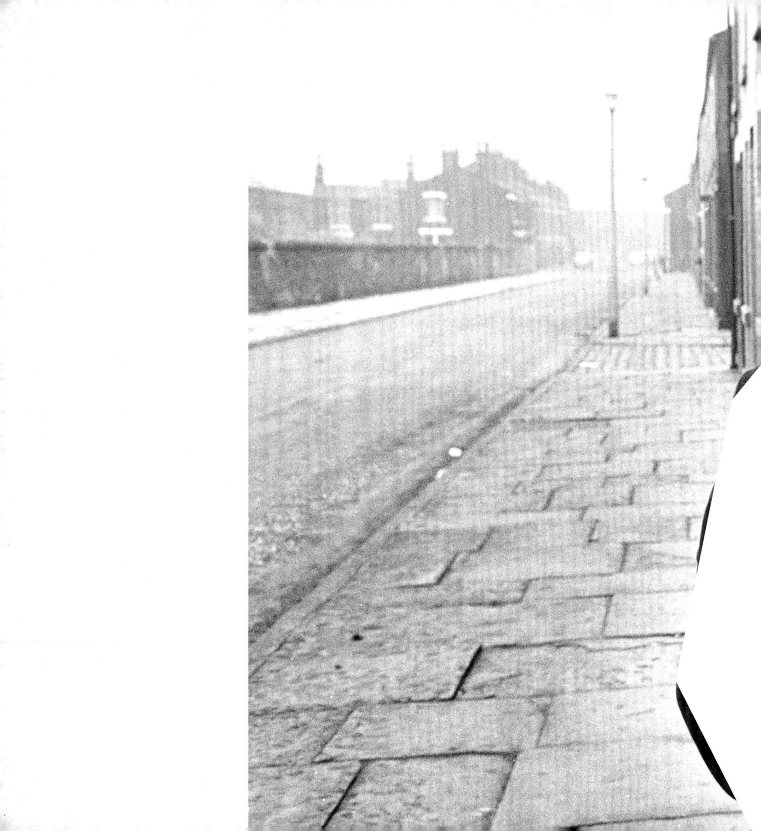

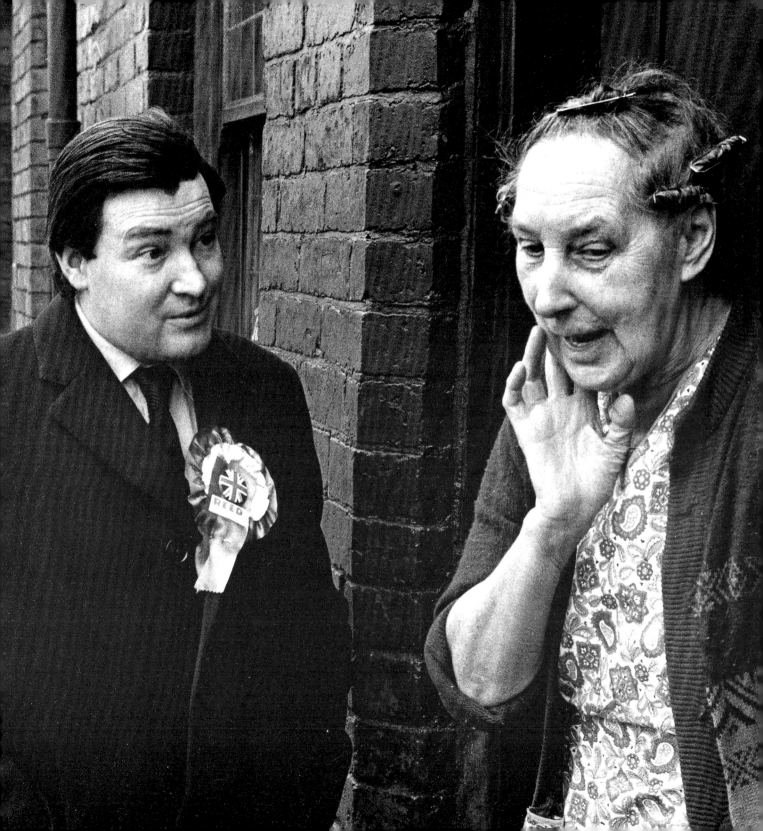

p. 6
*Airport Lounge* (location and date unknown)
The Hulton Deutsch Collection

p. 7
Vanley Burke, *Boy with Flag*, c.1969
Courtesy the artist

p. 8
*Constituent and Conservative Candidate,*
*Bolton East, General Election Campaign,*
February 1974
The Hulton Deutsch Collection

p. 11
*Visitors at Snow White's Castle, Eurodisney,*
*near Paris,* July 1995
The Hulton Deutsch Collection

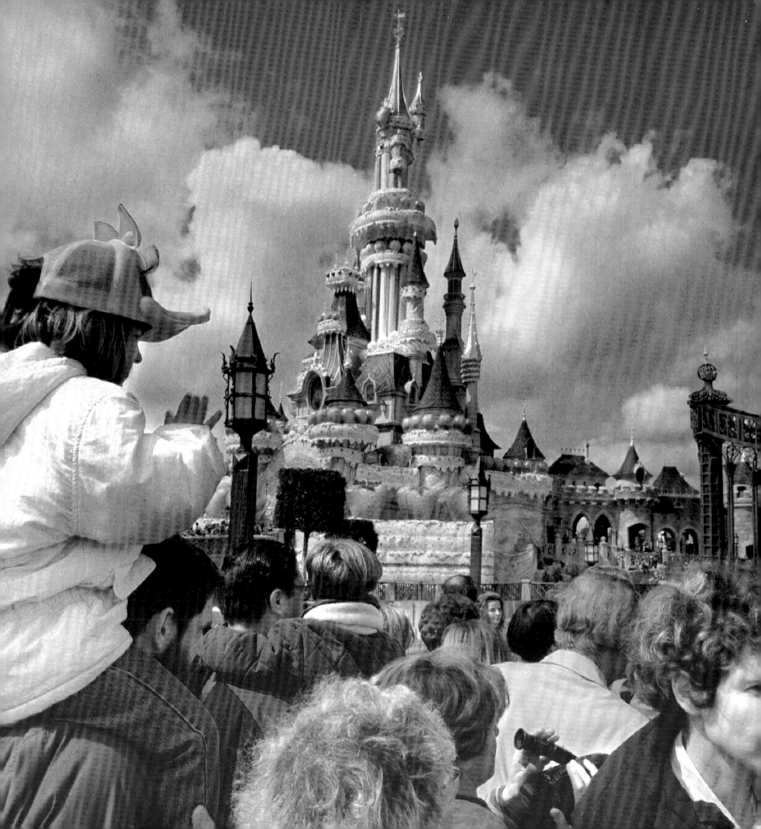

# Imagine All the People:
## Constructing Community Culturally
# Kobena Mercer

Everyone would like to be in one, but nobody is quite sure exactly what it is. 'Community' is a curious word. Constantly evoked to suggest a condition suffused with warm, fuzzy feelings and yet always eluding hard and fast definitions, its vagueness lends itself to all sorts of uses. The local council taxes me in order to provide services for the community; hospitals release patients to be cared for in the community; twelve nation states are said to constitute the European Community. The same term can be made to mean different things in as many different contexts: in each case it is the ability to invoke an ideal or imagined state of affairs that would seem to account for the elastic connotations of this one little word.

To be part of a community implies a kind of belonging that is more wished for than actually achieved, a feeling of connectedness that is more dreamed of than materially attained. And it is this wishing and wanting that makes community something that matters to almost all of us. 'Community' has come to be a keyword of contemporary life, not because we all live in one but because most of us do not: it is the lack of it that makes it valued, it is the loss of it that makes it desired, it is the envisioning of it that makes it real.

Bringing together diverse points of entry into an ambiguous and elusive idea that pervades contemporary culture, *Imagined Communities* offers a glimpse into the multi-faceted dimensions of what community can be. The footsteps of the industrial masses inscribed in Giuseppe Penone's sculpture recall history's past, while the paintings generated from statistical surveys by Komar and Melamid anticipate virtual communities to come. Between Denzil Forrester's figurative rendition of diaspora culture and Christian Boltanski's remem-

orative assemblages, whose flickering light bulbs illuminate the coils of collective memories, we can see how the notion of community has a mercurial flow, touching upon different structures of feeling as it courses through the social body.

The intriguing thing about community is the way the same term brings people together and, almost always, tears them apart: it is both a point of convergence and a point of contention. Gillian Wearing's photographs can create a strange kind of pathos out of their participatory ambience; while Gary Simmons' investigations into the toxic mythologies of 'race' in popular culture reveal a visible source of corrosive divisions.

Tim Rollins + K.O.S. form a kind of interpretive community by way of their collective practice, while Sophie Calle has brought out the most idiosyncratic of stories from chance encounters made possible by the anonymity of the modern city. In its fluidity of possible meanings, the multi-accentual aspect of community features in the textiles used by Yinka Shonibare: made in Europe and yet made to mean Africa, the Dutch wax-print fabric actually originated in Indonesia. This hybrid history singularly encapsulates the complex diversity of the cultural spaces we inhabit imaginatively at the end of the twentieth century − communities that are criss-crossed by the trans-national movement of cultures, ideas and people across the boundaries we use to identify the emotional ties of belonging.

The exhibition's title calls to mind Benedict Anderson's influential study of the modern nation as the *locus classicus* of 'imagined community', and there are two of his key themes which seem particularly salient to contemporary art in an era when nationalisms of whatever stripe are being called into

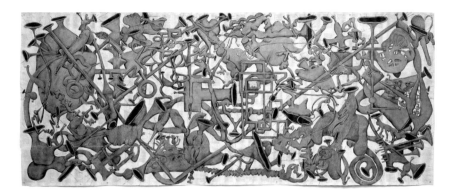

fig. 1
Tim Rollins + K.O.S.
*Amerika 1*, 1984–85
Oil stick, acrylic and charcoal
on book pages on rag paper
182 x 439 cm
Chase Manhattan Bank, New York
Courtesy Mary Boone Gallery, New York

question. Acknowledging the difficulty political science has had in reaching a consensus on what the phenomenon of nationalism actually is, Anderson's insightful move was to examine its cultural roots in nineteenth-century Europe, which led to the view that nations come into existence through society's collective imagination:

> *It is imagined because the members of even the smallest nations will never know most of their fellow members, meet them, or even hear of them, yet in the minds of each lives the image of their communion.* [1]

Looking at the role of print-media, such as newspapers, in shaping national identities, Anderson's response to the question − what are the materials with which communities imagine themselves into being? − drew attention to the primary role of representations. Like the national flags, anthems and even postage stamps that provide further evidence of 'the invention of tradition', [2] the cultural history of nationalism reveals processes of representation which are formative, rather than merely reflective. Art has been especially important in framing images of nationality (with state patronage of portraitists and history painters), and it is no surprise to see artists play an influential role in shaping what could be called forms of counter-nationalism whose existence is imaginative or even spiritual, and not necessarily attached to the ownership of territory or property.

'No nation now but the imagination', said Derek Walcott, the St Lucian poet whose words echo lyrically into the rhythmic dynamics of Denzil Forrester's paintings. In works such as *Carnival Dub*, 1984 (cat. 4), Forrester's depictions of

ensemble scenes saturated with the presence of music do not so much document as deepen an artistic dialogue about the communal experiences they describe. Music has been of signal importance in forging community out of uprooted histories of dispersal, for, as philosopher Cornel West describes it:

> *New World Africans are deeply modern in the sense of being exiles, banished from their native lands and forced to live lives as perennial 'outsiders', finding a 'home' in a dynamic language and mobile music − never in a secure land, safe territory or welcome nation.* [3]

Spinning layers of pulsating form and colour around grouped figures in works such as *Domino Hunters*, 1985 (cat. 5), Denzil Forrester's painting bears witness to the social contexts, as diverse as music or sports, in which communities of the Caribbean Diaspora have recreated themselves culturally. As in other works by black British artists, such as *Cricket Days, Domino Nights* (1986) by Sonia Boyce, there is something for everyone to celebrate in the underlying cultural dynamic whereby disparate elements come together to issue hybrid moments of unanticipated originality. Reggae, originating from Jamaica in the 1960s, was not only adopted in English pop in the 1970s, but has since become the lingua franca of African pop music, from Ras Kimono in Nigeria to Lucky Dube in South Africa. In place of rigid dichotomies, the aesthetics of hybridity enables the recognition of ethnicity as an inevitable part of anyone's cultural identity.

Amongst post-modern counter-nationalisms, which detach the emotional ties of belonging from the territorial claims of

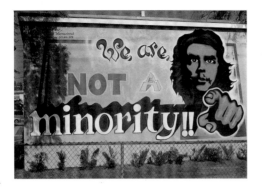

fig. 2
Congresso de Artistas Chicanos en Aztlán
(Mario Torero with Zapilote, Rocky, El Lton, Zade)
*We Are Not A Minority,* 1978
Mural
Approx. 6 x 9 metres
Estrada Courts Housing Project, East Los Angeles

the nation state, such reinventions of tradition have engendered alternative ways of imagining the rights and duties of citizenship. When hip-hop animateur, Afrika Bambatta, proposed the Zulu Nation as a name for collective loyalties and elective affinities amongst multicultural youth in the early 1980s, he was using a set of aesthetic and ethical principles that could also be found at work in the interventions of Queer Nation, whose clarion call – 'We're here, We're queer, Get used to it' – resounded through the late 1980s to assert the universal ordinariness of lesbian and gay identities. [4] In this connection, Keith Haring's distinct pictographic code offers a vivid instance of how visual culture contributes to building a sense of imagined community.

Haring's anthropomorphic sign-language moved across various sites, from subway stations and commercial advertising to the Gay Community Center in New York, creating what demographers would call a 'psychographic' map which linked individuals into a network by the recognition of coded signs. Taking into account his initial involvement in the Wild Style era of New York grafitti art, as well as other practices which blur the boundaries between public culture and community art, such as the 1970s' Los Angeles mural movement (fig. 2) led by Mexican-American artists like Judith Baca [5], 'community' could be said to be a verb not a noun – something you do rather than something you own.

However, although visual culture can effectively create imagined community – as seen with the red or blue cotton handkerchiefs used by LA gangs – such boundary markers of identity and difference are inherently volatile. There has been much discussion in contemporary culture of otherness as a necessary component of identification, yet often the relatively simple, albeit paradoxical, matter of the structural interdependence of Self and Other gets overlooked. Gary Simmons' *Us and Them* (1990), comprising two bath towels, placed side by side on a rail, each monogrammed with one of these words in gold lettering, brings interdependence back into the field of vision by deftly substituting the gender clichés of the 'his 'n' hers' matching towel set with the colour-coded clichés of 'racial' confrontation. With supple irony, Simmons brings out the discrepancy in common-sense reasoning whereby sexual difference is imagined in terms of complementarity, while racial difference is visualised as a polarity, even though both systems overlap in marking symbolic boundaries of differentiation.

If community is felt to be a universal value because it carries human dreams for unanimity and reconciliation, the other side to the story of modern nationalisms lies in exclusionary histories based on fantasies of sovereignty which seek to deny or downplay human interdependence. Acknowledging the powerful emotional forces which motivate nationalism, Benedict Anderson touches on themes of mortality when he suggests that the nation

*...is imagined as a community, because, regardless of the actual inequality and exploitation that may prevail in each, the nation is always conceived as a deep, horizontal, comradeship. Ultimately it is this fraternity that makes it possible, over the past two centuries, for so many millions of people, not so much to kill, as willingly to die for such limited imaginings.* [6]

The grim realities of fratricide amongst rival gangs such as the LA Bloods and Cripps (who formed a truce after the 1992 uprisings), reveal the tragic side to the enduring myth of sovereign self-sufficiency, which can only result in the wish to eliminate the Other (upon whom one nevertheless depends for one's sense of identity). If communities come to be united mostly in moments of tragedy and grief, art itself is always involved in rituals of mourning and remembrance which make reparations for the damage done by trauma and loss.

Christian Boltanski uses found materials, such as the suitcases, gloves, coats and other mislaid personal possessions in *Lost Property* (1994), or fading photographs arranged in metal boxes in *The Reserve of the Dead Swiss* (1994), to navigate the opacity of collective memory and explore the enigma of the unknown Other. The lost objects are imbued with a density of feeling all the more affective on account of the absence of information about their original owners. The photographs elicit curiosity about the untold stories behind the anonymous portraits and, in the face of such unknowing, what Boltanski brings to light are the im-pulses which inform the scrutiny we give to images of absent ones, whose absence is felt by the potent reminders they leave behind. Public ceremonies associated with the tomb of the unknown soldier gain emotive power precisely because their actual contents are empty or unknown. Even when named, as in the Vietnam Memorial Wall in Washington DC, such structures elicit depth of feeling by bringing us into the realm of the unrepresentable. Working on a further demonumentalised scale, Boltanski draws out charged responses from the banal and pathetic objects which, none-theless, bear witness to the human need for remembrance.

Absence, and the sculpting of form from the material traces of the past, is also evoked by Giuseppe Penone's *Contour Lines*, 1989 (cats. 8-11). Based on casts from the Dean Clough factory in Yorkshire, the staircase becomes a testament to the masses of workers whose footsteps created its flowing contours. Once a mill for the production of luxury carpets, built between 1841 and 1869 – the era of industrial modernity at its peak – it was closed down in 1982 to become, for almost a decade, an archaeological ruin in the wastelands of a post-industrial society.

The perception that modernity is a thing of the past may suggest that this may be an era of post-nationalism, although the contemporary resurgence of neo-nationalism implies otherwise. *Et pluribus unum?* Traditional formulae for binding heterogenous masses into the homogenous space-time continuum of the nation state have splintered under the local and global developments that were never anticipated by the founding fathers of the Enlightenment. In the often dystopian spaces of the post-modern public sphere, symbolic divisions have intensified as social mobility reduces to mere journeys between television, motorway and shopping mall, where atomised individuals follow routes with minimum social contact.

Based in the South Bronx, Tim Rollins and the Kids of Survival formed the Art & Knowledge Workshop Studio to answer their circumstances by means of collaborative strategies. As an art teacher, Rollins has worked with groups of African-American and Latino-American teenagers to develop a co-operative working method in which canonical texts are visually reinterpreted in the light of the collective

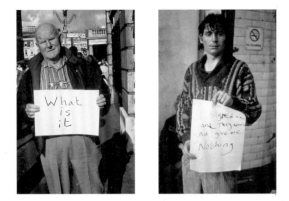

fig. 3
Gillian Wearing
From *Signs that say what you want them to say and not signs that say what someone else wants you to say*, 1992-93
Cibachrome on aluminium
30 x 17 x 1 cm
Courtesy Interim Art

knowledge and experience of the group. In *Amerika 1*, 1984-85 (fig. 1), Kafka's novel inspires a medley of horn-like shapes to orchestrate an allegorical revision of the American Dream as a source of both harmony and cacophony. With the book's pages as the canvas, the text literally becomes the ground upon which fragmented mythologies of national identity come to be reconfigured.

The expatriate Russian artists, Komar and Melamid, also work collaboratively on issues arising from the political indeterminacy of *demos* − the fact that the democratic identity of 'the people' is never fixed by a left/right binary code. *America's Most Wanted* (1994) and *Most Unwanted* (1994) are paintings based on market research, a method repeated in Russia and other countries as part of their ongoing project called *The Most Wanted Paintings* (cat. 7). The similar results, showing a preference for landscapes and distaste for abstraction, might confirm the view that populist taste inevitably equals parodic kitsch, although Komar and Melamid also raise questions about the public accountability of art and artists in societies which hold that the common good can always be delivered by the laws of the market-place.

With an altogether different approach, Gillian Wearing enters the anonymity of urban crowds to arrive at a participatory aesthetic that is happy to accept the vagaries of individual quirks as inadvertent points of collective contact. In the photographic series in which she asks strangers to reveal their innermost thoughts (and proclaim their democratic rights to a voice), Wearing elicits hilarious responses which are funny because they find empathic rapport with the pathos of the ordinary which they provoke.

The series' full title − *Signs that say what you want them to say and not signs that say what someone else wants you to say*, 1992-93 (fig. 3) − encapsulates a post-ironic ethos of participation in which the artist refuses a privileged place and also implicates the viewer, by inviting recognition of the ways in which, in the face of the unknown or anonymous, we often fill in uncertainties with our own identifications. Like Boltanski's *Children of North Westminster Community School*, 1992 (cat. 1), Gillian Wearing's vox-pop exerts a certain fascination by playing with this persistent identificatory response to contingent encounters − if these are anonymous images of everyone and anyone, then it could be you!

Sophie Calle also uses anonymity as a starting point for inquiry into the instabilities of the public/private boundary. Since early work such as *The Sleepers* (1979), for which she invited strangers to share her bed and then documented their stories, or *The Hotel*, 1981 (cat. 2), in which she pretended to be a chambermaid, taking photographs of the rooms of absent occupants, Calle has elaborated narratives in which she acts as a detective, working with the traces, clues and memories of someone or something that is no longer there. Yet, as the aim of the pursuit, the unknown Other is more an object of curiosity or even desire than of fear or paranoia, which more often predominate as key emotions in the encounter with the Stranger.

'Hell is other people', or so Jean-Paul Sartre once said; but Other People need not necessarily mean only anguish for His Majesty the Ego. Once the fragile threads of human interdependence are acknowledged, the space of imagined community becomes an occasion for enjoying the

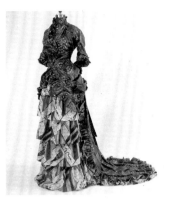

fig. 4
Yinka Shonibare
*How Does a Girl Like You Get to be a Girl Like You?*, 1995
Costume made of wax print cotton textiles
169 cm tall
The artist

unanticipated pleasures of surprise. Yinka Shonibare's *Double Dutch* (1992) and *Sun, Sea and Sand*, 1995 (p. 51) installations each feature jazzy fabrics whose fluid history shows that one is always implicated in otherness (fig. 4). In Africa the fabric has the allure of imported goods which are made in Europe, while in Europe itself the vibrant texture connotes exotica. In another twist, other West African textiles such as kente cloth from Ghana are now appropriated in popular fashions among young black people in the Diaspora. In other words, you may already 'belong' to communities that you previously did not even know existed.

Community is probably an inescapably universal human value because mortal individuals need to believe they belong to something that goes beyond their finite edges. Anthems are especially effective in creating imagined community musically, by using rhythm and harmony to invoke a transcendent feeling of 'unisonality'.

William Blake's *Jerusalem*, like *Rule Britannia* or *Land of Hope and Glory*, can inspire such shared structures of feeling – in much the same way that *The Star Spangled Banner* performed by Jimi Hendrix in 1969, or the Sex Pistols' dissident *God Save the Queen* released during the 1977 Silver Jubilee, are polyvocal soundbites from an era in which nationality fell apart as an agreed-upon basis for organising the human need for belonging. The persistent appeal to the imagination as a transgressive space of possibility – the utopian space that John Lennon sang about in *Imagine*, his paen to 1960s' idealism – may seem obviously awkward or hopelessly naïve in a new world (dis)order in which uncertainty is often felt to be the only thing that people share

in common. Yet far from being exhausted, the inarticulate wishing, yearning and imagining that drives the desire for connectivity would seem to be confirmed by the singing and dancing shoppers in Gillian Wearing's video-bloopers. As the artist acknowledges, history has an open-ended capacity for change:

> When I said I hated the eighties what I meant was I hated eighties materialism... As for the sixties and seventies, I do envy certain things then. People felt that they had a context and felt idealistic. Nothing lasts forever. Every generation re-makes itself. [7]

Notes

1 Benedict Anderson, *Imagined Communities: Reflections on the Origins and Spread of Nationalism* (London, Verso, 1983), p. 15

2 See Eric Hobsbawm and Terence Ranger (eds.), *The Invention of Tradition* (Cambridge University Press, 1983)

3 Cornel West, *Keeping Faith: Philosophy and Race in America* (New York, Routledge, 1994), p. xiii

4 See Lauren Berland and Elizabeth Freeman, 'Queer Nationality' in Michael Warner (ed.), *Fear of a Queer Planet: Queer Politics and Social Theory* (Minneapolis, University of Minnesota Press, 1993)

5 See Eva Sperling Cockcroft and Holly Barnet-Sanchez (eds.), *Signs From the Heart: California Chicano Murals* (California, Venice, Social and Public Art Resource Center, 1990)

6 Benedict Anderson, op. cit., p. 16

7 Gillian Wearing in Caryn Faure Walker, 'Signs of the Times' [interview], *Creative Camera*, Issue 332 (February/March 1995), p. 37

# List of Works

Dimensions are in centimetres,
height x width x depth

## Christian Boltanski

1   *Children of North Westminster Community School*, 1992
144 photographs on board
30 x 20 each
Courtesy Lisson Gallery, London

## Sophie Calle

2   *The Hotel #24*, 1981
Diptych with colour photographs and text
204 x 142
Private Collection, courtesy Fred Hoffman Fine Art, Santa Monica

3   *The Blind #17*, 1986
Colour photographs and text
150 x 120 x 10
Fonds National d'Art Contemporain

## Denzil Forrester

4   *Carnival Dub*, 1984
Oil on canvas
305 x 396
The artist

5   *Domino Hunters*, 1985
Oil on canvas
213 x 366
The artist

6   *B-Side Skank*, 1994
Oil on canvas
214 x 244
The artist

## Komar and Melamid

7   *The Most Wanted Paintings*, 1994 ongoing
A project adapted for the World Wide Web
at Dia Center for the Arts, New York
http://www.diacenter.org/km/index.html

## Giuseppe Penone

8   *Contour Lines I*, 1989
Iron, glass and sand
250 x 250 x 15
The artist

9   *Contour Lines II*, 1989
Iron, glass and sand
250 x 250 x 15
The artist

10   *Contour Lines III*, 1989
Iron, glass and sand
250 x 250 x 15
The artist

11   *Contour Lines IV*, 1989
Cast iron
224 x 115 x 54
The artist

## Tim Rollins + K.O.S.

12 *Animal Farm - G7*
*Animal Farm - New World Order*
*Animal Farm - Big 3*, 1989-92
Acrylic and book pages on linen
122 x 183 each
Mottahedan Collection, courtesy Mary Boone Gallery, New York

13 *Scarlet Letter IV*, 1991
Acrylic and book pages on linen
274 x 264
Collection Janet de Botton, London

14 *The Frog (after Aristophanes)*, 1995
Acrylic and book pages on linen
142 x 193
The artists

## Yinka Shonibare

15 *Five Under Garments and Much More*, 1995
African fabric, Rigilene, fishing line, interlining
Tailored by Sian Lewis
95 x 130 circumference each
The artist, commissioned by National Touring Exhibitions and
Oldham Art Gallery

## Gary Simmons

16 *Bones and Bows*, 1992
Paint and charcoal on masonite and oak
122 x 152
Courtesy Galerie Philippe Rizzo, Paris

17 *Swingin'*, 1992
Charcoal and paint on masonite and oak
122 x 152
Courtesy Galerie Philippe Rizzo, Paris

18 *Photo-Installation*, 1993
Latex on canvas and Polaroids
244 x 244 each
The artist, courtesy Metro Pictures, New York

## Gillian Wearing

19 *Dancing in Peckham*, 1994
Video installation
Dimensions variable
Courtesy Interim Art

20 *My Favourite Track*, 1994
Compilation videotape (edition of 5)
Approximately 90 minutes
Courtesy Interim Art

21 *The Regulators' Vision*, 1995
Video installation
Dimensions variable
Courtesy Interim Art, commissioned by National Touring
Exhibitions and Oldham Art Gallery

# Select Bibliography

Benedict Anderson, *Imagined Communities: Reflections on the Origins and Spread of Nationalism* (London, Verso, 1983)

Christian Boltanski, special issue, *Threshold*, No. 11 (Oslo, National Museum of Contemporary Art, 1994)

*Sophie Calle, à suivre* [exhibition catalogue], (Musée d'Art Moderne de la Ville de Paris, 1991)

*Sophie Calle, absence* [exhibition catalogue], (Rotterdam, Museum Boysmans-van Beuningen, 1994)

Germano Celant, 'Interview with Giuseppe Penone' in *Giuseppe Penone* [exhibition catalogue], (Bristol, Arnolfini, 1989)

Douglas Crimp, *On the Museum's Ruins* (Cambridge, Massachusetts, M.I.T. Press, 1993)

Marko Daniel, 'Art and Knowledge Workshop, A Study' in *Tim Rollins + K.O.S.* (London, Riverside Studios, 1988)

Tim Rollins + K.O.S., special issue, *Parkett*, No. 20, 1989

Mark Durden, 'Christian Boltanski', *Art Monthly*, January 1993

Paul Gilroy, *There Ain't No Black in the Union Jack* (London, Century Hutchinson, 1987)

Jeffrey Kastner, 'Christian Boltanski at Lisson Gallery', *Frieze*, January-February 1993

John Lyons, *Dub Transition, Denzil Forrester* [exhibition catalogue], (Preston, Harris Museum and Art Gallery, 1990)

Nancy Marmer, 'The Uses of Contradiction, Christian Boltanski', *Art in America*, October 1989

Kobena Mercer, *Welcome to the Jungle. New Positions in Black Cultural Studies* (London, Routledge, 1994)

Gregor Muir, 'Gillian Wearing at Interim Art', *World Art*, November 1994

Philippe Piguet, *The Eroded Steps* (Halifax, Dean Clough, 1989)

Andrew Ross, 'Poll Stars', *Artforum*, January 1995

Adrian Searle, 'Gillian Wearing at Interim Art', *Frieze*, September-October 1994

Yinka Shonibare, 'Purloined Seduction' in *Seen Unseen* [exhibition catalogue], (Liverpool, Bluecoat Gallery, 1994)

*Directions. Gary Simmons* [exhibition catalogue], (Washington D.C., Hirshhorn Museum and Sculpture Garden, 1994)

Julian Stallabrass, 'Power to the People', *Art Monthly*, April 1993

Sharon Waxman, 'A Sense of Solidarity, Christian Boltanski', *Art News*, May 1994

Frank Whitford, 'Snap Judgements', *The Sunday Times*,
25 October 1992

Peter Wollen, 'Painting History' in *Komar and Melamid*
[exhibition catalogue], (Edinburgh, Fruitmarket Gallery and
Oxford, Museum of Modern Art, 1985)


## Photographic Credits

Photographers:
Susan Crowe (pp. 41, 43),
Jack Dabaghian/Reuters (p. 11),
Steve Rees (p. 17),
Stephen White (pp. 26, 50)

p. 7:
Print supplied by Autograph, The Association of
Black Photographers

p. 14:
Photograph made available through Social and
Public Art Resource Center, Venice, California, USA

pp. 41, 43:
Photographs lent with kind permission by the
Henry Moore Institute, Leeds

# The Artists

Texts by Richard Hylton

Christian Boltanski

# Komar and Melamid

*Born 1944, Paris*
*Lives and works in Paris*

*I want my art to be like a mirror. Everyone who looks
at it sees himself, but every reflection is different and the
artist holding the glass up doesn't exist any more.
There is never a clear meaning or moral. You arrive at
enlightenment yourself.*
Christian Boltanski

Christian Boltanski's photographic installation, *Children of
North Westminster Community School*, 1992 (cat. 1),
involved the artist taking on the role of school photographer
in a school opposite the Lisson Gallery, to photograph the
new year's intake. The 144 portraits were displayed in
identical grid formation in both the school and gallery, and
the photographs were also sold to each of the parents.

In the school and in the hands of the parents, each pupil is
recognisable as an individual and the photographs function
as cherished mementoes of a personality. In the gallery,
the images take on a new meaning, becoming an
anthropology of adolescence. The simple shots of the
children are reminiscent of the anthropological use of
photography dating back to the nineteenth century, whereby
constructions of a social hierarchy based on notions of
normality and deviancy, from the criminal to the physically
disabled, were created. The meaning of the image and the
artist's intention are ambivalently poised, suggesting that
both are, in the end, reliant on context and the subjective
viewpoint of the onlooker.

Boltanski frequently draws from his personal stockpile of
images borrowed from friends and found in second-hand
shops, ranging from family snapshots to newspaper
photographs of murderers and victims. This approach
and the resulting allusions to childhood, innocence, death
and memory, have been leitmotifs throughout his work.

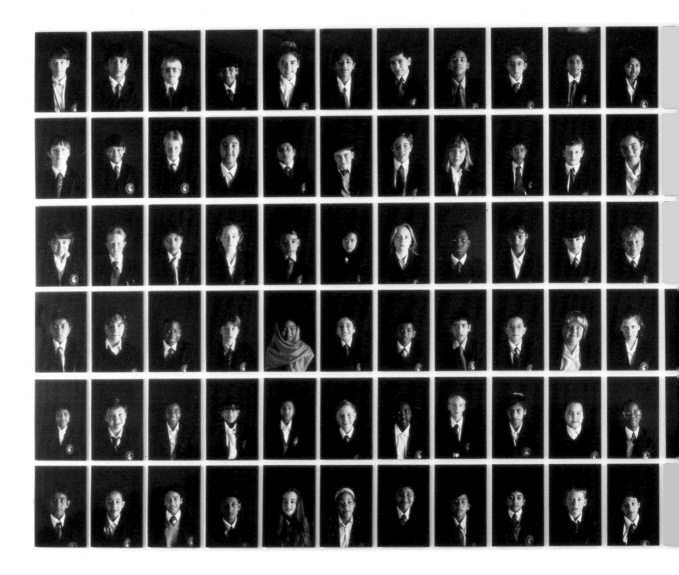

1
*Children of North Westminster Community School*, 1992

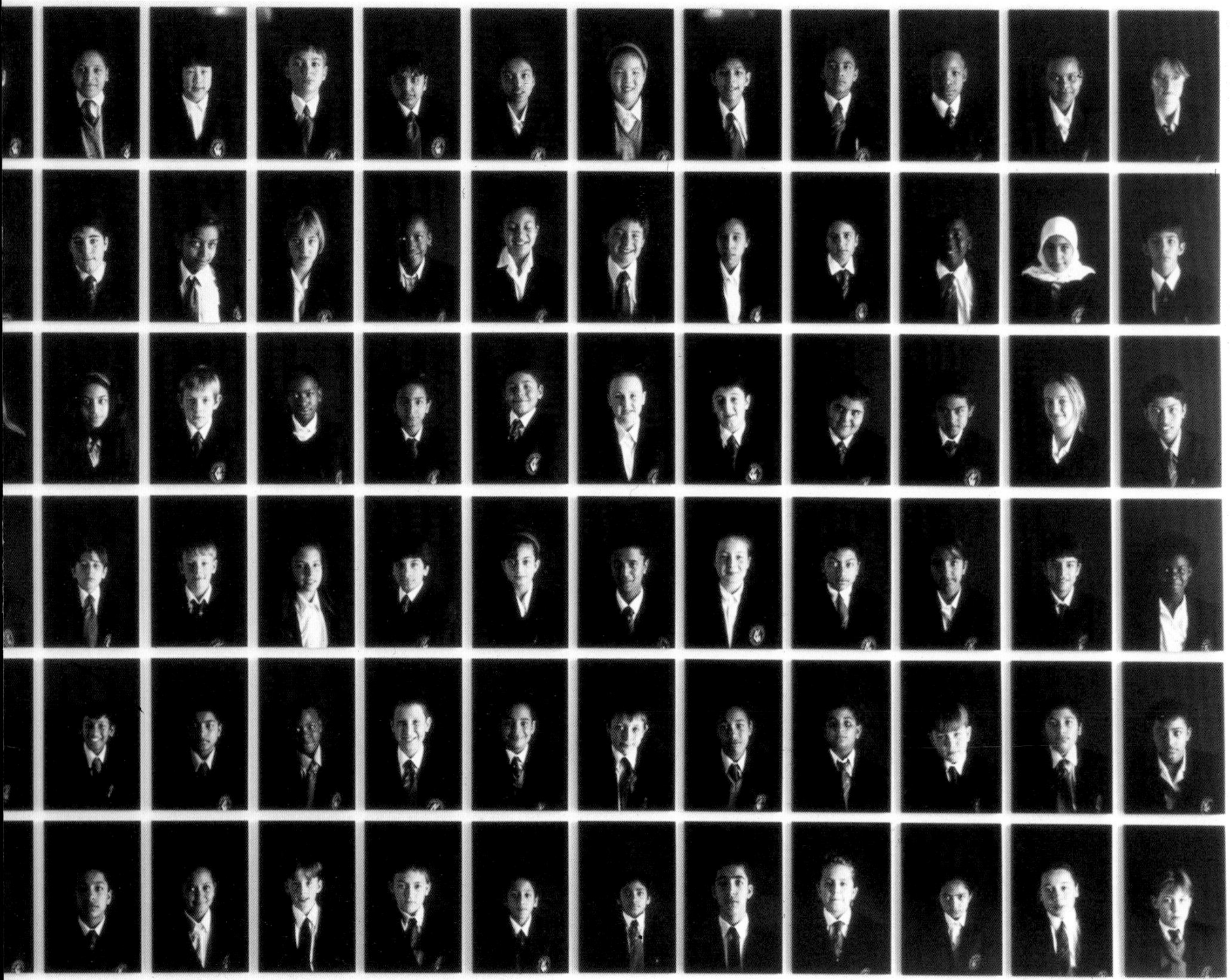

Sophie Calle

*Born 1953, Paris*
*Lives and works in Paris*

*The Hotel*, 1981 (cat. 2) is a photographic installation which involved Sophie Calle becoming a chambermaid in a hotel in Venice for a month. During this period, the artist secretly unpacked the occupants' personal belongings, arranged and photographed them, and recorded her observations:

*On Monday March 2 1981, 10.30 am I go into room 24, the pink one. The twin bed had been slept in. A strange feeling of 'déjà vu' comes over me. Various images blend together. Days and clients all run together in my mind. Haven't I already visited these? ... I empty the handbag on the floor: sugar cubes, tampax, pink lipstick, postal cheques made out to Paulette B, old tickets for a Xenakis concert and an agenda on the first page I read 'In the event of my death, everything I own will go to Mr François G exclusively' Signed Paulette B in a childish, touching handwriting.*

For *The Blind*, 1986, (cat. 3), Calle, as she herself describes it, '...met people who were born blind. Who have never seen' and '...asked them what their image of beauty was'. She then produced a portrait of each of the twenty-three participants, to accompany their descriptions and her photographic illustrations of their descriptions.

Sophie Calle's installation work crosses the traditional boundaries which define the role of the artist as a neutral observer of society. Reversing (visual) culture's traditional roles of men as voyeurs and women as their subjects, Calle implicates herself within her work. She deals with aspects of our lives which would normally remain private for reasons of transience or taboo.

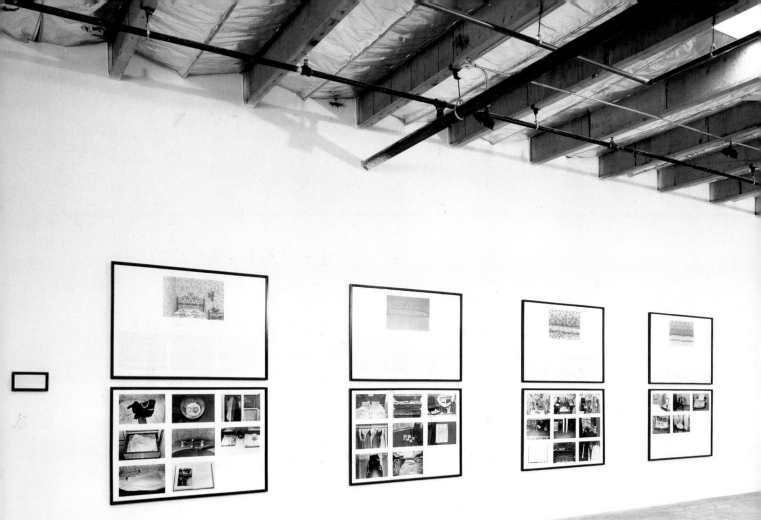

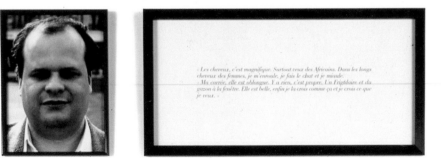

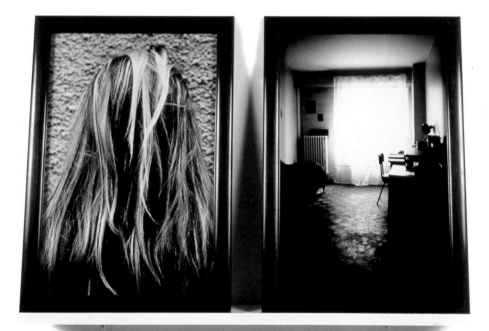

above
3
*The Blind #17*, 1986

left
2
*The Hotel*, 1981
Installation at Fred Hoffman Fine Art

# Denzil Forrester

*Born 1956, Grenada*
*Lives and works in London*

*As a young child in the West Indies, Carnival was an essential part of everyone's life and the memories of crowds, noise and movement, still vivid in my mind, are revealed in my painting. Coming to London was a big change, no nature, the earth was damp, the atmosphere dark, and full of houses. These two very different islands, one colourful, the other seemingly dull, awakened me visually and led me to want to create images from both worlds.*

John Lyons, 'Dub Transition' in *Caribbean Expressions* [exhibition catalogue], (Leicester Museum and Art Gallery, 1986), p. 21

Denzil Forrester graduated from the Royal College of Art in 1983. He has portrayed a variety of subjects in his paintings, including blues and reggae clubs in London. This work was influenced by his passion for dub and reggae music through the 1980s. The night-clubs became his second studio, where he would produce initial studies for his paintings. His earlier work on Carnival combined celebratory and utopian feelings, as can be seen in the monumental *Carnival Dub*, 1984 (cat. 4). *Domino Hunters*, 1985 (cat. 5) reflects on the police's intrusion on and intimidation of the black community, the theme of an earlier work, *Funeral of Winston Rose* (1982), which Forrester painted as a memorial to his friend, who died under suspicious circumstances whilst in police custody. His painting style combines African and European aesthetics, in addition to the influences and memories of his native Grenada.

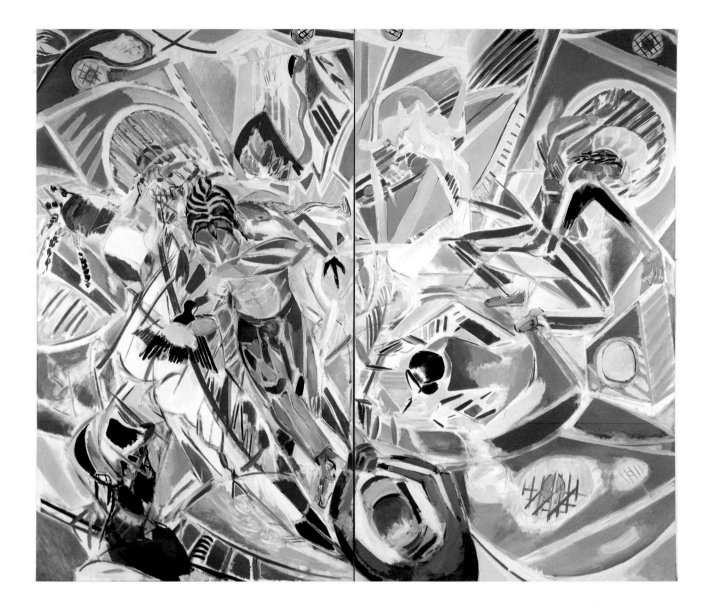

4
*Carnival Dub*, 1984

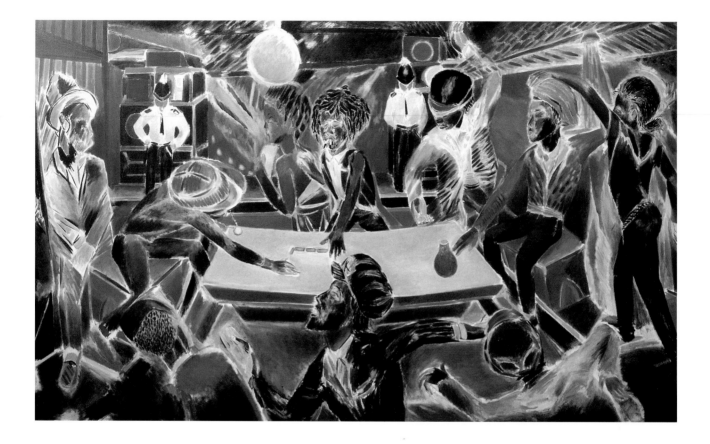

5
*Domino Hunters*, 1985

*Vitaly Komar, born 1943, Moscow*
*Alexander Melamid, born 1945, Moscow*
*Both live and work in New York*

Komar and Melamid base *The Most Wanted* and *Most Unwanted Paintings* on statistical information derived from the results of marketing surveys conducted in different countries by professional PR companies. The surveys began in America and Russia and have extended to China, Denmark, Finland, France, Germany and Scotland. They seek the responses of a cross-section of society to questions on a range of issues such as lifestyle, personal values and aesthetic judgement.

*America's Most Wanted* and *Russia's Most Wanted Paintings* reveal very telling similarities and differences between the two countries' attitudes towards art. The sweeping landscape and the family are replicated in both the American and Russian paintings. Moreover, the fact that both Americans and Russians chose iconic figures, albeit of a different nature (George Washington and Jesus, respectively), suggests a similar view of cultural values.

*The Most Wanted Paintings* project highlights how society generally sees art as functioning autonomously and separately. The survey – commonly a mainstay of politicians, the media and the market-place – is here applied to art production, which is traditionally held to be influenced by notions of genius, technique and individual expression. The seemingly conscientious and methodical way in which Komar and Melamid set about their 'duty' contradicts the 'populist' view of contemporary art as élitist and irrelevant to the majority. In providing the public with 'what they want' and by presenting a 'banal art' based on majority preferences, the artists mock the critics of contemporary art projects, and

their funding. Komar and Melamid use irony and humour to expose overriding notions of taste, value and attitudes towards art, at the same time highlighting the function of the survey method as a tool for social conditioning. Taken a step further, *The Most Wanted Paintings* are now available on the World Wide Web Internet, which opens up the possibility of creating an international people's painting.

You can respond to Komar and Melamid on their Internet site at the following address:
http://www.diacenter.org/km/index.html

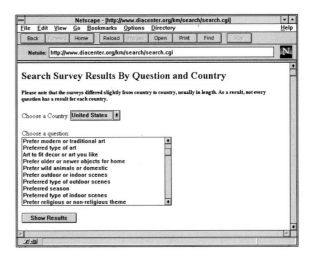

7
Page from *The Most Wanted Paintings*, 1994 ongoing

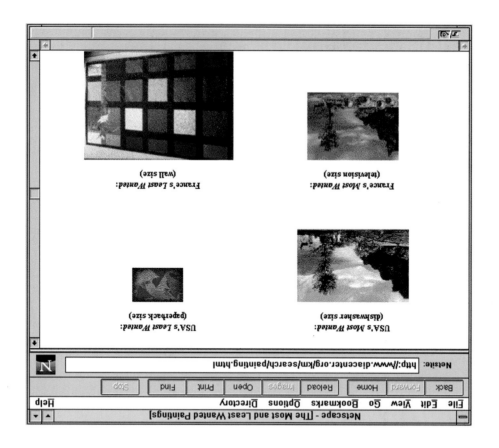

7
Page from *The Most Wanted Paintings*, 1994 ongoing

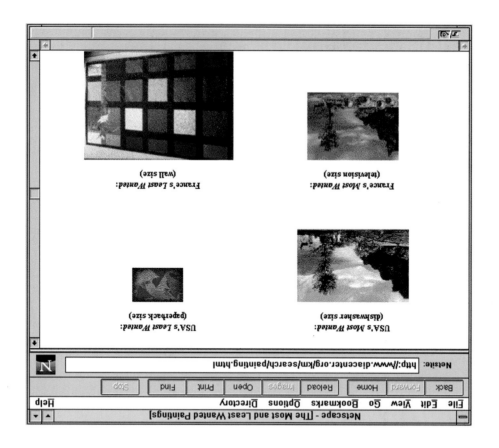

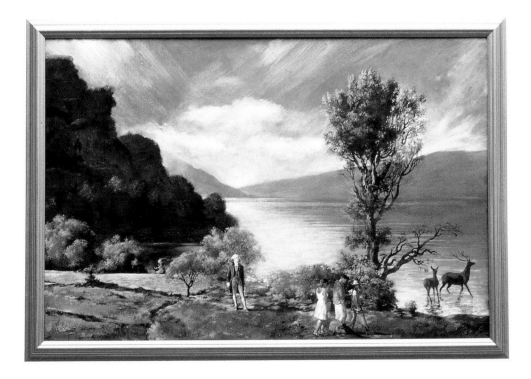

*America's Most Wanted*, 1994
Oil and acrylic on canvas, 61 x 91 cm
The artists

# Giuseppe Penone

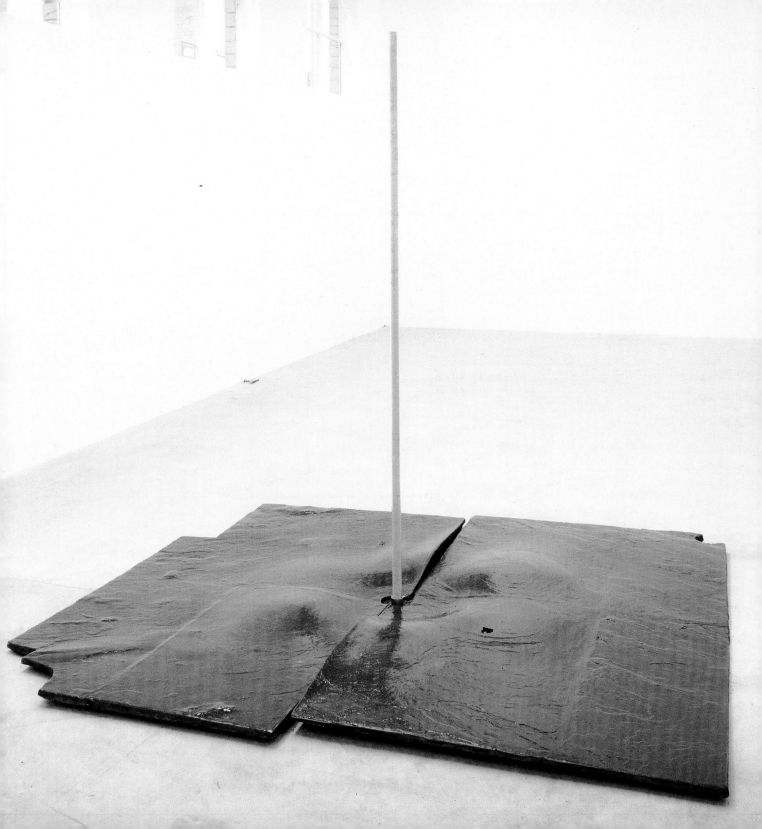

*Born 1944, Garessio, Italy*
*Lives and works in Turin*

*An industrial site, symbol of a revolution and of the striving*
*ambition of a family empire, a complete town dedicated to*
*the conception of technological progress, living to the rhythm*
*of machines – a fantastic waging of civilisation. A different*
*landscape; one of factories, mills, workshops, warehouses.*
*An active landscape where the monuments are linked to the*
*very nature of the place, to the production from its belly.*
Philippe Piguet, 'The Eroded Steps' in *Contour Lines* [exhibition catalogue],
(Dean Clough, Halifax, 1989)

Giuseppe Penone's sculpture is commonly associated with
the relationship between the human body and nature. His
work utilises a wide variety of animate and inanimate natural
forms and elements including trees, leaves, stones, water and
their immediate environments. Their surfaces, texture, lives
and deaths are explored in minute detail. Linked to these
studies are Penone's explorations of the relationships
between parts of the human body, which he has carried out
over the last twenty years. He takes imprints from his own
body and – using walls, glass, adhesive tape or gelatin
substances (as in *Eyelids*) – draws parallels between the
body's surfaces and its transformations and natural forms.
As the artist explained when interviewed by Germano Celant
in 1986 (Arnolfini, Bristol, p. 19), he magnifies these 'maps'
of the body and transfers them to canvas and stone, thereby
revealing 'unknown territory'. His imprints of fingers and
elbows examine human surfaces, areas which leave traces of
contact but which we scarcely think about: 'I had made the
gesture of touching – an insignificant, everyday action with
nothing special about it' (Penone quoted by Philippe Piguet,
*The Eroded Steps*, op. cit., p. 20).

Penone was invited to Dean Clough, in Yorkshire, to produce
works based within the mills, now redundant, which used to
manufacture luxury carpets. *Contour Lines* consists of a
number of cast-iron mouldings of the mills' staircases and
landings. Penone selected the oldest staircase from one
of eight mills and 'imagined the crowd of people passing
here to reach their work place' (Penone quoted by Philippe
Piguet, *The Eroded Steps*, op. cit., p. 20). In *Contour Lines*,
Penone continues to explore his fascination with the
interaction between the human body, space and surface.
Here the individual body has been replaced by a mass of
millworkers who have left their imprints on the staircases
and landings in which they worked. The 'work' was created
by the millworkers and delivered to us by the artist. This
memorial to a community now gone contrasts sharply with
the sanitised image of Britain's industrial past commonly
presented by the heritage industry.

previous page
8
*Contour Lines I*, 1989

opposite
11
*Contour Lines IV*, 1989

Both works photographed at the exhibition
*Contour Lines* at the Henry Moore Studio,
Dean Clough, Halifax, 1989

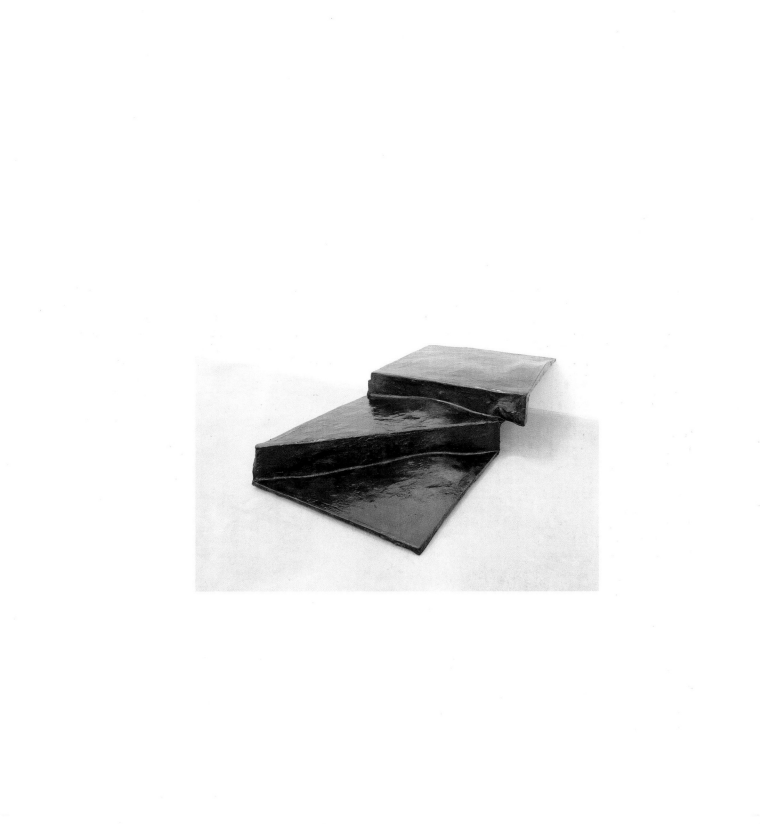

# Tim Rollins + K.O.S.

*Tim Rollins, born 1955, Pittsfield, USA. K.O.S. has included Angel Abreu (born 1974), George Abreu (born 1979), Christopher Hernandez (born 1978), Victor Llanos (born 1975), Nelson Montes (born 1972), Carlos Rivera (born 1971), Nelson Savinon (born 1971), Lenin Tejada (born 1974). Tim Rollins + K.O.S. are based in New York.*

*The art objects we make are vital things, but they are still only trophies – culminations of a learning process and a collective radical will. Art is most important to us as a means to knowledge.*

Tim Rollins + K.O.S. interviewed by Marko Daniel, February 1988 (from Marko Daniel, 'The Art and Knowledge Workshop: A Study' in *Tim Rollins + K.O.S.*, Riverside Studios, London)

Tim Rollins was hired, in 1981, to teach art to teenage students in the South Bronx who were deemed 'learning disabled' and were from economically disadvantaged African and Latin American communities. By 1982, the classroom had turned into a 'working studio for young artists' and Rollins began to concentrate all his art practice within this group. The art sessions took place during free periods, lunch breaks and short sessions after school. As the enthusiasm for the art sessions grew, Rollins and the Kids of Survival moved into a disused gymnasium in the South Bronx, which became the Art & Knowledge Workshop. The group, consisting of about twenty members, would meet after school and at weekends.

Their working method usually involves Rollins selecting a 'Classic' work of literature, which each individual reads and then discusses collectively, relating the literature to their own experiences within an economically deprived community. The group largely concentrates on painting, pasting the pages of their chosen novel to a canvas and superimposing their 'collective' image. The paintings range from literal 'translations' of novels such as Orwell's *Animal Farm* to more conceptual interpretations, such as that of Nathaniel Hawthorne's *Scarlet Letter*. Their use of canonical texts is part of Rollins' strategy within the community context:

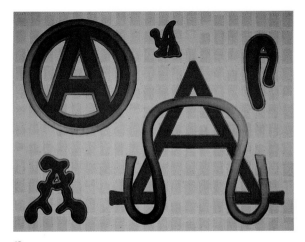

13
*Scarlet Letter IV*, 1991

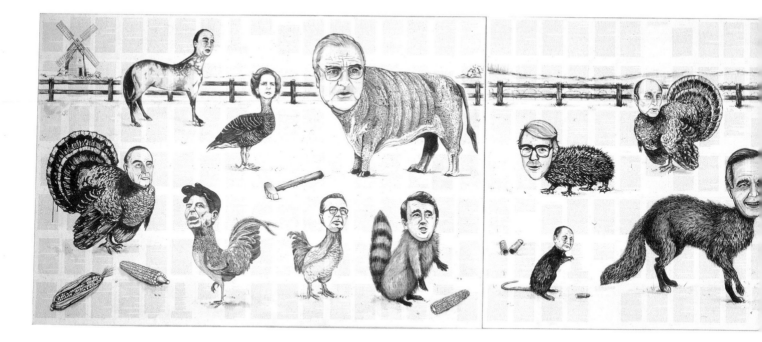

12
*Animal Farm – G7*
*Animal Farm – New World Order*
*Animal Farm – Big 3*, 1989-92

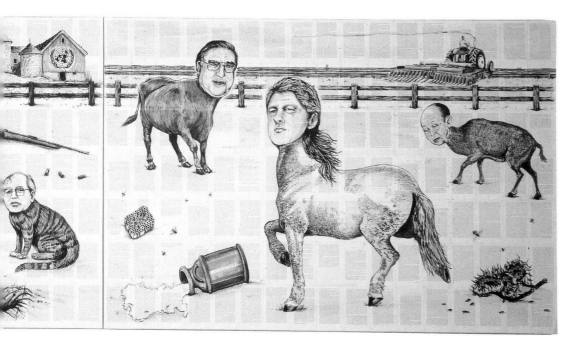

*The capitalist system is a total system. So to do anything you are going to have to play to the rules a little bit. Either that, or you don't really want to win the game.*
Tim Rollins + K.O.S. interviewed by Marko Daniel (ibid.)

Financial success has enabled members in K.O.S. to take up scholarships. The project has provoked a mixed reaction from artists, curators and historians. Besides earning broad critical acclaim, it has been greeted by some with scepticism regarding the political significance of a white artist working with Latino and black American youngsters from socially deprived communities:

*As everyone knows (but few are willing to articulate), the art world would not have reacted so positively to K.O.S., if a fresh scrubbed, young, white artist (who had worked with conceptual artist Joseph Kosuth and co-founded Group Material) had not been their figurehead.*
Dan Cameron, *Parkett,* No. 20, 1989

The group's identity is shaped by those external forces which shaped the neglected Bronx community. The activities are currently split between the school based in the Art & Knowledge Workshop and the Kids of Survival art project.

Yinka Shonibare

*Born 1962, London*
*Lives and works in London*

*African fabric: signifies African identity, rather like American Jeans (Levi's), an indicator of trendy youth culture. In Brixton, African fabric is worn with pride amongst radical or cool youth. It manifests itself as fashion accessory with black British women in the head wrap form and it can also be found worn by Africans away from the home country. It becomes an aesthetic of defiance, an aesthetic of reassurance, a way of holding on to one's identity in a culture presumed foreign or different.*

Yinka Shonibare, 'Purloined Seduction' in *Seen Unseen* [exhibition catalogue], (Bluecoat Gallery, Liverpool, 1994), p. 15

*Black Britain defines itself crucially as part of a Diaspora. Its unique cultures draw inspiration from those developed by Black populations elsewhere. In particular, the culture and politics of Black America and the Caribbean have become raw materials for the creative processes which re-define what it means to be black, adapting it to distinctively British experiences and meanings. Black culture is actively made and re-made.*

Paul Gilroy, *There Ain't No Black in the Union Jack* (Century Hutchinson, London, 1987), p. 154

Yinka Shonibare continues his work with African fabrics in *Five Under Garments and Much More*. In presenting corsets ornately tailored in African fabrics, he questions a multiplicity of cultural assumptions pertaining to history, identity and 'belonging.' The corsets are reminders of an eighteenth-century aristocracy whose opulent lifestyle was based on colonialism and its resulting displacement of millions of Africans. The combination of under-garments and African fabrics suggests an array of connotations, ranging from the 'ethnic' and exotic to the sexual and seductive. However, Shonibare challenges the colonial tradition whereby the 'other' was made a subject of fascination and the hierarchical relationship between the coloniser and colonised was institutionalised. The assimilation of the fabric into current black British cultural expression is irrevocably linked to the days of Empire and the contemporary Diaspora. The fabrics have been used to represent many identities from African Nationalism, imported from the USA, to the 'ethnic' which exoticises African-ness. These identities are further called into question by the origins of the fabrics which came first from Indonesia and are now manufactured in Britain and Holland, to be sold in places such as London's Brixton Market, but are also, ironically, exported in bulk to Africa. Shonibare wittily questions the linearity of history and identity, exploding the myth that cultures exist as mutually exclusive entities.

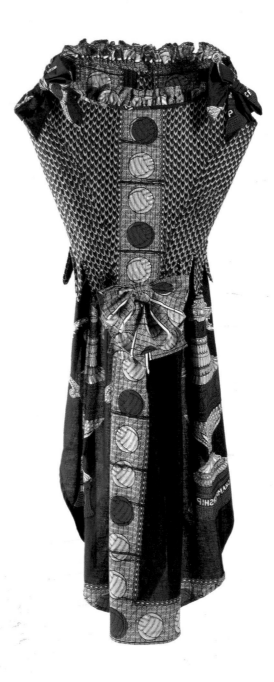

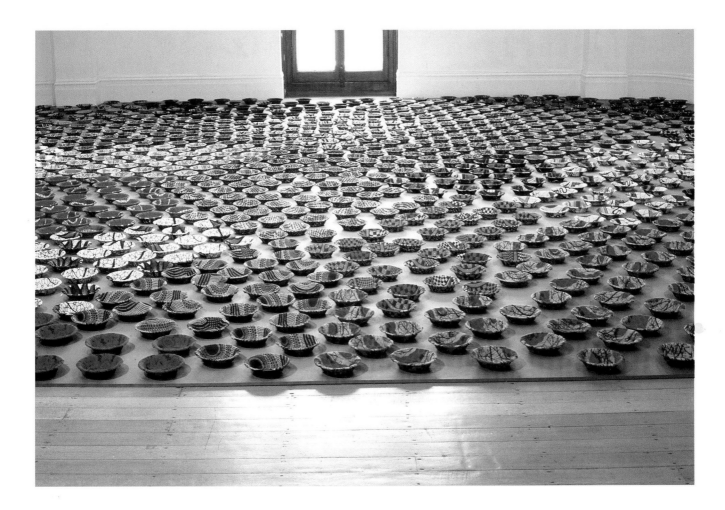

opposite
15
*Five Under Garments and Much More*, 1995

above
*Sun, Sea and Sand*, 1995
Mixed media installation at BAC, London
Dimensions variable
The artist

Gary Simmons

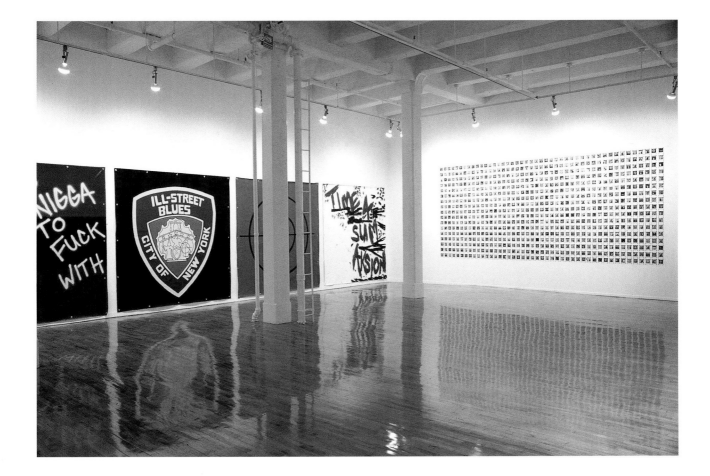

18
*Photo-Installation*, 1993
at Metro Pictures, New York

*Born 1964, New York*
*Lives and works in New York*

Gary Simmons focuses on the power wielded by America's popular culture industry in manufacturing black stereotypes and role models. Simmons' chalkboard drawings are part of the series *Erasure*, which comprises thirty works focusing on the depiction of black people in cartoons by Walt Disney, Walter Lantz and Max Fleischer. Presented on chalkboard, as a metaphor for learning, the drawings refer to cartoons which we absorb from infancy and which form part of our 'early unconscious entrance into the world of racial ideas' (Simmons interviewed by Amad Cruz, *Directions* [exhibition catalogue], 1994). Simmons re-presents the characters and objects, stripped of their original animated setting and retaining only the symbols of racial subordination. The drawings exist in a physically fragile state, vulnerable to permanent erasure, abandoning the relative permanency of the film medium. Ironically, obliteration would only superficially destroy the drawings' pernicious existence, which in reality is etched deep into our psyches.

Simmons' installation draws on elements of African-American youth culture to highlight its distance from mainstream popular culture in America. Image and text combine graffiti and graphic styles, reworking familiar iconography central to rap music and Afrocentric culture. Expressions such as 'Original Man', 'Fat Pockets', 'wrong nigga to fuck with' and 'Roots' adorn the slick emblematic backdrops which Simmons erected at street locations in Brooklyn and Harlem. Inviting passers-by to pose in front of a painting of their choice, Simmons produced two polaroids – one for the volunteer to keep and one to be used for the gallery installation, which finally comprised a total of 850 polaroids. The portraits and emblematic paintings reveal the double-edged existence of African-American youth culture: although this culture is increasingly embraced by society as a whole, albeit often in ignorance of its contemporary significance, the community from which it originates remains marginalised from mainstream society.

54

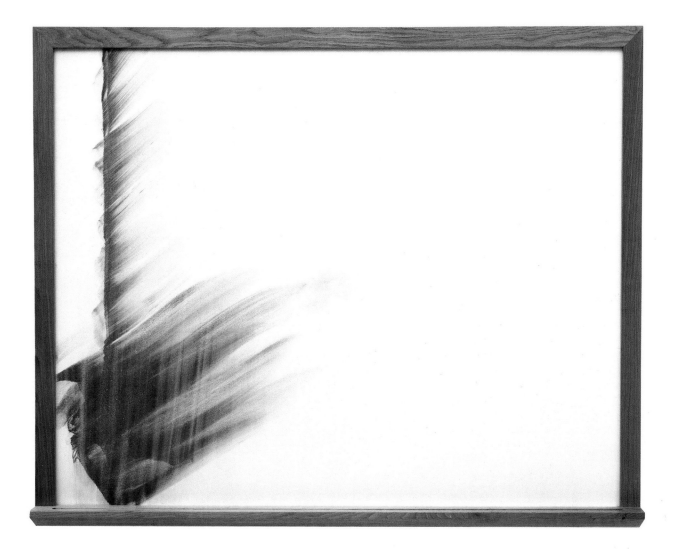

17
*Swingin'*, 1992

Gillian Wearing

*Born 1963, Birmingham*
*Lives and works in London*

Gillian Wearing's face to face encounters with strangers, who become both her performers and audience, create an intimate and eclectic urban anthropology of human behaviour. *My Favourite Track*, 1994 (cat. 20) involved the artist going out on the street, approaching members of the public who were listening to music through headsets, and inviting them to sing their favourite songs on video camera.

The willing participants' atrocious attempts at singing are offset by the video piece *Dancing in Peckham*, 1994 (cat. 19), which features Wearing in the uncomfortable position of dancing silently in front of a static video camera in a shopping centre to memorised songs, such as Gloria Gaynor's *I Will Survive* and Nirvana's *Smells Like Teen Spirit*. This self inflicted 'performance' suggests that Wearing is, above all, interested in the relationship between artist, audience and gallery rather than 'taking the piss out of' her performers.

For *The Regulators' Vision*, 1995 (cat. 21), a specially commissioned work, Wearing has cannibalised her video piece *Western Security* (1995), in which she turned her attention from street subject-matter to the interior of an empty building. For those 'in the know' the space is the Hayward Gallery; for those who are not, the function of this undisclosed space is unclear. *Western Security* features a cowboy shoot-out, not in Hollywood Technicolor movie style which mythologised the cowboy as the aborigine of the American West, but recorded in black and white on ten surveillance cameras. Dressed in full regalia, the cowboys and cowgirls scurry to and fro, creating a cacophony of gunfire. Wearing, dressed in cowgirl costume, sits stranded,

tied to a chair and gagged, awaiting her liberators. The dead are wrapped in bubblewrap and taken away by uniformed security guards who are oblivious to the frenetic scampering of the cowboys.

Originally presented on ten separate monitors, the performance has been reduced for *The Regulators' Vision* to one monitor with a composite image of the ten screens. The performers are here displayed via a video wall projection, and watch their own performance from a living room. The spectacle now becomes us watching them, watching 'them'. The gallery, once the site of a cowboy spectacle, returns to its mainstay function, as a place for the display of art.

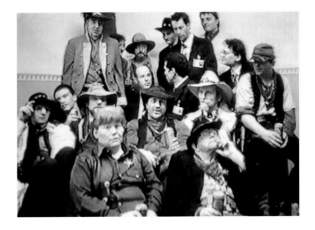

21
Still from *The Regulators' Vision*, 1995

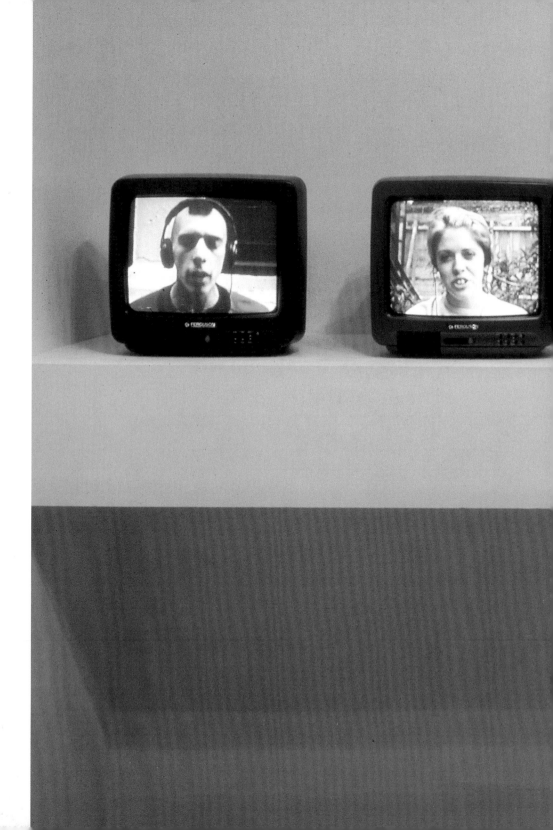

20
*My Favourite Track*, 1994

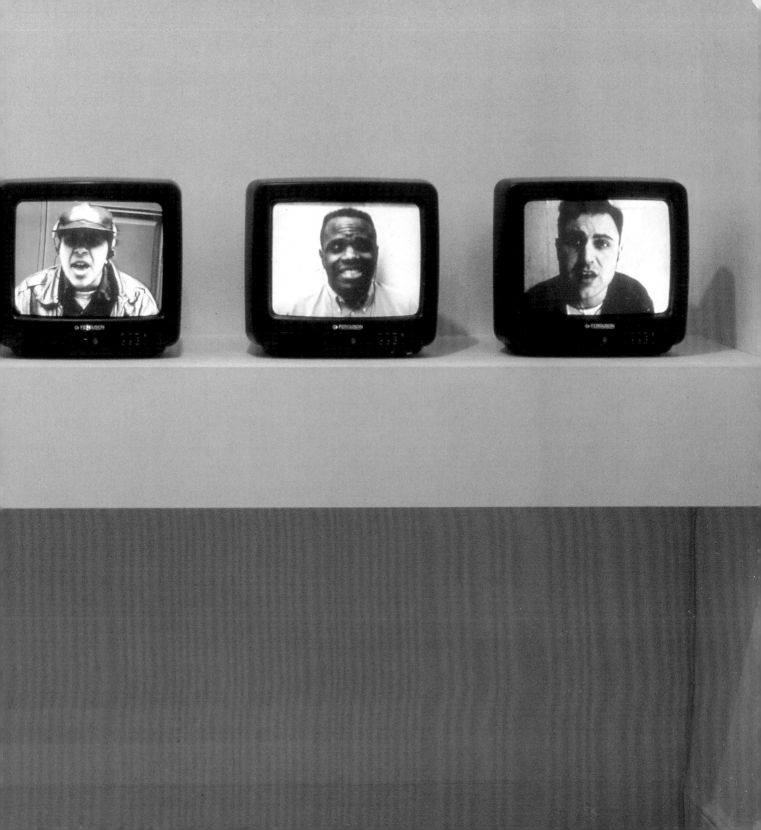